The Fruit Trees Book: Growing Apples – A Beginner Gardening Books Series
Yard Upkeep, Soil Testing, Planting, Pruning and Tree Care

VAS BLAGODARSKIY

Copyright © 2018 Vas Blagodarskiy

All rights reserved.

ISBN: 1-949727-01-7
ISBN-13: 978-1-949727-01-2

DEDICATION

I'd like to say big thanks to my grandmother Svetlana and my great-grandmother Galina who ran the country house orchard that inspired me to write this book. I'd like to dedicate this book to them. I hope it will inspire in the reader a lifelong interest in growing apples.

Special thanks to my editor Becky.

Special thanks to all the patient tree owners who taught me what I know.

Special thanks to Amazon for helping to distribute my book.

Thank you all!

Vas Blagodarskiy, Author

Vas Blagodarskiy

CONTENTS

DEDICATION iii
CONTENTS v
ACKNOWLEDGMENTS vii
Welcome To Your Ultimate Guide To Growing Apple Trees! 1
Twenty of the Most Popular Apple Varieties of All Time 13
Red Delicious 14
The McIntosh 16
Pink Lady 18
Cripps Pink Apples 20
Ambrosia Apples 22
Crispin (Mutsu) Apples 24
Braeburn Apples 26
Granny Smith Apples 28
Cameo Apples 30
Honeycrisp Apples 32
Paula Red Apples 34
Empire Apples 36
Jazz Apples 38
Yellow Delicious Apples 40
Gala Apples 42
Fuji Apples 44
Jonagold Apples 47
Macoun Apples 49
Cortland Apples 51
Diva Apples 53
More Hints for Growing Healthy Trees 56
ABOUT THE AUTHOR 63

ACKNOWLEDGMENTS

This book finds people at the right place and at the right time. Typically, a person doesn't go out of their way to read a book on apple growing, unless they have some kind of urgent interest in the matter. Having said that, I hope my book scratches whatever itch you may be experiencing right now. Perhaps you want to feel pride of ownership by growing your own orchard. Or maybe you want to make people smile when they drink your fresh-squeezed apple juice. Whatever the case may be for you, please remember to leave this book 5 stars once you've gotten value from it, so other people like you can discover it for themselves.

Vas Blagodarskiy

WELCOME TO YOUR ULTIMATE GUIDE TO GROWING APPLE TREES!

While professional apple growers have learned traditional, time tested ways to get the most from their apple orchards, most of us are hobbyists who simply enjoy the taste of a fresh off the tree apple.

There are many reasons people grow apple trees in their own backyards or smaller groves and orchards. The ability to make fresh apple sauce or pies or just grab a tasty treat right off the tree are just a few.

If you've chosen to grow apples yourself, you will soon learn that it can be rewarding and (as most rewarding things in life are) somewhat difficult.

This detailed guide to growing your own apple trees will cover nearly everything you need to know, from planting the young seedlings to harvesting apples from a matured tree. I will cover special considerations for choosing a variety of tree that best suits your needs, and the best ways to care for your trees to encourage them to grow strong and healthy so they can consistently yield delicious fruits.

Diseases, pruning, special care for grafted trees, thinning the fruit, and much more will be covered in this guide. In addition, I will present you with twenty of the most popular apple varieties and their specific needs.

A Few Time-Tested Tips from Professional Apple Growers

Many generations of apple growers have used simple guidelines to ensure the success of their orchards. These tips are handy for the professional grower as well as the hobbyist.

1. Protect Your Trees with Paint:
To protect their trees from chemical damages from weed killers and pesticides, professional growers will paint the bottom of their trees. They apply the paint with a glove or a rag. Once the trees are coated with protective paint, the growers can safely spray weed killer or other chemicals.

2. Cut Low Branches:

To encourage the tree to produce fruit on the top branches, a professional will cut all growth and branches from the tree to under around thirty inches above the ground. This is also a way for them to keep the trees growing upwards, and not into each other.

3. Wind Machines For Frost Protection:

Frost can be deadly to an orchard. Even one late frost can ruin all the trees overnight. Professional growers will use windmills, known as wind machines, to keep air moving on cold nights. When air is moving between the trees, it becomes warm enough to keep frost at bay.

4. Ground Level Sprinklers For Frost Protection:

While it seems a strange concept, sprinkling the trunk of the trees with water is a common way to protect them against frost. Even though it would seem that an ice-covered tree trunk would be even colder, the ice coating itself acts as a protection against frost. Professional growers do not use overhead sprinklers because of the risk of the trees developing diseases; these sprinkler systems are lower to the ground.

5. Pluck Blooms To Avoid Fire Blight:

Fire blight can destroy a nursey full of young trees without warning. This disease happens when young apple trees get water, from sprinklers or rain, into their delicate blossoms which then get exposed to hot conditions. Fire blight is highly contagious to other trees, so even one infected tree can wreak havoc on a young orchard. Since this only happens when the trees are blooming, professional growers will remove blossoms from them if rain is expected. This results in a slower growth time, but the trees will grow strong rather than dying off because of fire blight.

6. Drip Irrigation Systems:

Many growers prefer to use a drip irrigation system instead of an overhead sprinkler system to protect the trees from fire blight and other diseases. These irrigation systems are kept one foot above the ground to protect them against damage that can be caused by mowing or animals.

7. Reflective Tarps To Have A Uniform Harvest:

A reflective tarp will mirror light back into the apple trees so that the bottom of the growing fruit will be exposed to it. This practice results in the apples ripening together and having an even coloration.

8. Support For Growing Trees:

Young trees need extra support against damaging wind. Apple growers tie their young trees to trellises to keep them growing straight and strong. Tree trellises are stakes that are driven into the ground and secured to the tree with wire and twine.

9. Thin Clusters For Much Bigger Apples:

If you've ever been to an orchard, you've probably noticed a lot of apples laying on the ground among the trees. Professional growers will often thin out the harvest, encouraging the remaining apples to grow larger. Removing some apples will allow those still on the tree to get more of the nutrients they need.

10. Keep Weeds and Animals Away:

You're not the only one that loves a good, juicy apple. Many burrowing animals can hide in the weeds around your apple trees. These animals can do a lot of damage to the trees themselves as well as to your equipment. To keep pests away, make sure you get rid of the weeds around your trees.

11. Plant Trees Closer Together:

You can plant a larger number of trees in a more limited space if you maintain proper pruning techniques and give them trellises to grow on. Using this approach allows you to plant trees two to four feet apart rather than the conventional spacing of between seven and ten feet.

12. Orchard Grass Controls Weeds:

When you are growing apples, your focus should be on the trees themselves and not landscaping between the trees. Professional growers plant orchard grass around the trees to keep pesky weeds away. Orchard grass is a slow growing variety of grass that only requires mowing every few weeks.

13. Tree Grafts:

If the grower decides to change his apple variety in the orchard, he will cut the trees back to a few feet from the ground, grafting his preferred variety to the existing tree trunk. The new apple trees have a much better chance for survival because they are attached to an older tree with an established root system.

Planting Your Young Apple Trees

Because most apple trees come in three varieties, standard, semi-dwarf and dwarf, you can grow apple trees even if you don't have a huge plot of land.

Standard sized apple trees tend to require more maintenance and grow into large trees and harvesting the fruit can be difficult because of their height.

Semi-dwarf and dwarf apple trees are great for the apple growing hobbyist. They don't grow as large as the standard sized tree, making it easy to have more than one. Because they don't grow as tall as standard varieties, it is far easier to harvest their fruit.

Espalier trees are those varieties that are trained to grow flat against a surface and are very popular trees because they can be grown in very small areas.

A cultivar is a tree variety that has been developed using several species, each one with desirable traits such as growing seasons, sizes, and climate needs. This makes it easier for the grower to choose a perfect tree that meets his requirements for:

Blossoming and ripening seasons
Size and height of the tree at maturity
Soil needs for optimal growth
Space needed for growth of mature tree
Climate needed for the tree to thrive

Choosing the location to plant your apple trees can be a bit tricky. The most important feature of the spot you've chosen is continuous morning sunlight exposure. This is because dew collects in the young tree's blossoms and can lead to devastating diseases. Bright, warm sunlight will quickly evaporate the dew in the morning, keeping your tree safe from diseases such as fire blight.

To give your young apple tree the best chance to thrive, choose your site carefully.

Soil Type: The best soil for an apple tree will allow for excellent drainage. It should be moderately rich, and able to retain air and some moisture as well.

Mulch: Try mulching with organic materials such as straw or hay to retain the soil's moisture. Organic material will decompose, providing the tree with extra nutrients.

Support: Some varieties of apple trees, such as dwarf, can be so overladen with fruit that they uproot themselves. Apple trees should be supported with a stake or trellis, or be planted against a wall for support.

Sunlight: Apple trees love a bright, sunny location. They will do best on a northern or eastern facing slope that receives sunlight at least six hours or more all summer long.

Frost: Young apple trees are very susceptible to frost damage. Make sure the location you choose is high enough that cold air flows away from the site rather than into it. A lower lying site will be prone to frost.

Soil Testing: To ensure your apple trees are well suited for the location you have in mind, collect a soil sample. The Cooperative Extension Service can instruct you on how to collect the soil sample. They will also explain your testing results to help you make any adjustments to your soil that may be necessary, such as adjusting the pH of the soil or correcting nutrient deficiencies. These adjustments should be made to a depth of a foot or more below the bottom of the hole where you will plant the tree so the roots will continue to benefit from them as they grow.

Spacing: Your apple tree seedlings or established trees should be spaced between fifteen and eighteen feet apart. Dwarf trees can be planted closer together, between four to eight feet. The spacing required for apple trees will be determined by soil fertility, the amount of maintenance pruning you will be willing to do, and the apple tree variety itself.

Avoid the Woods: Apple trees do best if not planted near heavily wooded areas or other trees.

Other Planting Considerations

Generally, fall planting of young apple trees is not recommended unless you live in more temperate climates. Most central and northern areas are prone to freezes and frosts, sometimes into the early spring. If you're lucky enough to live in a location like Hawaii, you can plant the trees any time you like; for the rest of us, we should target spring as the best time for planting.

If the tree you choose is not in a dormant state and has leaves already growing for the season, it will be very susceptible to injury from:

Wind damage
Cold snaps
Late frosts
Temperatures above 90°F or below 50°F

These are common conditions in the early spring, but they can also occur throughout the year, depending on the climate of the area.

It is recommended to get established small apple trees from a local nursery. They will most likely be in plots when you purchase them, and you should leave them in their pots for several days.

Your trees will need to be hardened off, or acclimated, before you can plant them outside.

1. Start by placing them in a sheltered area during the day: Initially, leave the pots outside for no more than three to four hours a day for the first few days, gradually increasing their time outside by an hour or two each day. Find a sheltered spot for them, free of direct sunlight or damaging weather, and bring them back inside each night and between the outdoor exposures. Inside, the trees can be gently misted. Your location and weather conditions may prolong the hardening process.

Pay special attention to the leaves of your new trees. Leaf damage indicates that the plant is not acclimating well, and that it needs to start the acclimation process over again from the start.

Your location and weather conditions may prolong the hardening process

2. Move the pots from the shade to gentle morning sunshine: After a few days of being in the shade, move the trees into a spot where they can receive filtered morning sunlight, returning them back to their shady spot after a few hours. At this point, the apple trees still need to be brought inside at night. Remember to keep their roots wet by watering them if their soil seems dry.

Your potted trees should be hardened after a week and ready to move permanently to their outside locations, but only if the daytime temperatures remain between 50°F and 90°F. If these temperatures are going to change any time over the following days, it is better to keep them in their pots and continue the hardening process.

3. Wait a total of ten days: By day ten, provided the weather is cooperating, it's time to move your apple trees to their permanent spots. Plant them on a cloudy day, if possible.

Before planting the young tree in the ground, make sure its roots are moist. If the roots aren't moist, they should be placed in water before they are planted in the ground.

To plant the trees:

Clear an area about four feet in diameter. Make sure all grass and weeds are removed from the circle.

The hole should be about twice as wide as the root system, and approximately two feet deep. After digging the hole, throw some loose dirt back into it and loosen some of the dirt on the walls of the hole so that the root system can take hold easily. Spreading the roots out gently, place the young tree into the hole, making sure they aren't twisted as you cover them with soil. Pat the dirt firmly into place to fill in any air pockets.

Avoid adding fertilizer when planting your apple trees. The roots can become burned from fertilizer.

Most varieties of apple trees have been grafted. The area of the graft is called the scion, and this must be about 2 inches above the dirt. You can identify the scion by the appearance of swelling on the tree.

The trees must be watered regularly so they can establish a healthy root system.

Mulch can be replaced as needed for weed control, taking care that in the fall it is pulled away from the trunk of the tree. Mulch is the perfect nesting place for mice during the winter months, and they will snack on the bark of your young apple tree.

Once the tree is planted, it may take several years to yield fruit. It's important to maintain it throughout the entire growing process.

When choosing your apple trees, keep these things in mind:

Tree tags are not always a reliable source of information regarding the best growing conditions for the tree, but catalogs and the internet are. Additionally, you can contact the local Cooperative Extension Service to get recommendations for the best apple tree variety for your location.

Remember that not all apple trees are suitable for every environment.

Each variety of apple tree may have a different time frame to reach maturity and yield fruit.

All apple trees require a certain amount of time that they are exposed to temperatures between 32 and 45 degrees Fahrenheit to set fruit. This time frame is called "chill hours" and vary between tree varieties, depending on how far north they are. This protects the trees from a late freeze. Chill hour information is usually located on the tags, or you can ask the seller at the nursery for more information.

Tree varieties categorized as hardy will thrive when planted in Hardiness Zones 3 through five. Those categorized as long-season are best suited for Hardiness Zones 5 through 8.

Training And Pruning

Leaders are the main extensions of the trunk; all branches grow out from the leader, which is essentially the spine of the apple tree. Trees should be trained so they can grow tall, straight and strong. Dwarf variety apple trees should be trained to the central leader, while semi-dwarf and standard trees are trained to modified leaders.

Pruning is the best way to ensure that your apple tree grows in an orderly way. Left to their own devices, the trees grow branches randomly and fill with fruit. Even though this seems like a great idea as far as the quantity of fruit, the fruit itself will be smaller and unhealthy.

While young apple trees don't require much pruning, you should remove any branches that are dead or broken. Too much pruning of your tree will slow its growth and delay its ability to yield fruit. Instead of actively pruning, you can control a young tree's growth patterns:

If a branch is growing too rapidly, don't remove it. Tie it down to the ground nearly horizontally using stakes or fasten it to some lower branches. Keep it retrained for two to three weeks to slow its growth and encourage fruiting.

Gently rub off any buds that are growing in random spots on the young tree before they turn into untamed branches.

An apple tree is considered mature once it begins bearing its fruit. Mature trees require pruning at least once a year to control disease and encourage fruiting by thinning out branches, allowing air and light to get to the remaining branches and under the canopy. Mature trees should only be pruned when they are in their dormant cycle.

If a tree limb starts to decrease its yield, remove it so newer, healthier branches can thrive.

Remove any fruiting spurs, which are the smaller branches that never grow more than a half-inch or so yearly after the tree has reached ten years of age.

Remove stems that are growing upright, typically seen higher up in the tree

Cut back branches that are drooping and remove all weak stems, usually found underside the limbs.

Thinning the Crop

Fruiting apple trees experience a natural thinning of fruit called an annual spring drop, which usually happens in June. Four to six weeks after the tree blooms, however, you should thin out the apples to discourage pests and disease. The best time for thinning is generally when the fruit is about one half inch across, or dime sized. Ideally, you should try to leave between six to 8 inches between the apples buds. Thinning the trees will keep branches from breaking off from a heavy fruiting and ensure that the apples that are left will be larger and better tasting. After the first time the tree fruits for the year, thin the crop to get rid of any apples that are not growing well or are damaged. Leave approximately four inches between the fruits that remain, or approximately one apple per forty to sixty leaves, and check that the remaining fruit is spaced evenly on the branches.

Conditions That Can Affect Your Yield

Because your apple trees can have bad years, you should plant several even if the tree is of the self-fertilizing variety. Planting more than one tree ensures that you will have a steady crop of apples, even if one of the trees isn't yielding much fruit. It's also recommended to plant more than one tree if you are trying to grow a variety that is not recommended for your location.

Apple crops can be affected by poor weather. Storms can cause a tree to lose its blossoms, and cold weather may result in a poor yield or, in extreme cases, no crop at all.

If the tree produces too much fruit, it can place a serous strain on the tree. Too many large apples in a single season can lead to a diminished crop the next year.

If your apple tree is not producing blossoms and the weather has been good, it could be experiencing stress because of a lack of nutrients and water. Fertilizer and regular watering will correct this problem. Too much pruning or intense thinning of the tree can also result in a decrease of blossoms, indicating a poor harvest to come.

During the fall and through the winter, apple trees will stop fruiting and begin to go dormant. This makes fall the perfect time to plant mature trees so they will be easier to maintain and more likely to get a healthy start without having to undergo hot summer sunlight or having to produce fruit until they have become firmly established.

Disease Prevention

There are some diseases that can devastate your orchard quickly. The only defense is to stay vigilant for signs of them, and to keep your trees healthy. Make sure your tree is armed against disease by maintaining proper water levels, good fertilization, and adequate soil conditions. Apple trees are especially prone to several diseases, most commonly:

Cedar apple rust:

Cedar apple rust is a disease that strikes apple, cedar, and juniper trees. Once a tree is affected the disease cannot be stopped and it will spread to other trees.

Signs: Cedar apple rust will show on the tree leaves as small yellow or rust colored spots. It tends to strike in the late spring. Eventually, the tree will prematurely drop its leaves and its fruit.

Treatment: While cedar apple rust can't be controlled once it takes hold of a tree, you can prevent its spread by spraying fungicide on surrounding trees, especially if they are young and still growing.

Powdery mildew:

Powdery mildew will target both the leaves and the fruit of apple trees. The tree can be saved if it is caught in time, but if it isn't properly treated the tree's health will deteriorate.

Signs: Powdery mildew shows up as a white colored fungus on the fruit, blossoms, and leaves of the tree.

Treatment: To control powdery mildew, apply fungicide to apple trees in the early spring when the leaves are starting to grow.

Fire blight:

This is a bacterial infection that will kill the tree if left untreated.

Signs: Fire blight affected trees will have blackened branches that appear to be scorched.

Treatment: The best way to avoid fire blight is to choose a variety of tree that is resistant to it. If you see signs of fire blight on your trees, remove the affected branches.

Apple scab:

This is a fungus that strikes new leaves during wet weather, most commonly in the spring. It can also strike more mature leaves in late spring or early summer.

Signs: Apple scab shows as spots that look like black velvet on the leaves of your tree. As the disease progresses, the leaves will turn yellow and drop off the branches.

Treatment: You can prevent apple scab by choosing trees that are disease resistant. During the early spring, apply a fungicide before the leaves are fully out.

TWENTY OF THE MOST POPULAR APPLE VARIETIES OF ALL TIME

Apples come in many different varieties. Some have a very tart taste, while some are sweet. Apples can have subtle undertones of other flavorings, such as vanilla or berry, or be classically flavored with balances of tartness and sweetness. Many apples have a long shelf life, and some are more resistant to bruising and browning than other varieties.

Your choice of apple tree will depend on what flavors and balances you enjoy in your fruit as well as what you intend to use it for. While some are classically delicious in pies and baked goods, others do not stand up to heat and will lose their shape and flavor.

Here are twenty of the most popular apple varieties of all time with some information to help you choose what variety is best suited for your tastes and needs.

RED DELICIOUS

Size at Maturity:

20 to 25' high and 25' wide for standard. The semi-dwarf is smaller at 12 to 15' high and 12–15' wide while the dwarf variety will reach only 10' high and 10' wide.

Growing Climates:

World wide

Expected Yield Season:

September

***

The Red Delicious apple is the most popular variety in the United States. It has a taste that is sweet and mild, with very little tartness. It has a thick skin and a crumbly texture.

It is best for eating right off the tree; Red Delicious apples are generally not preferred in baking.

Red Delicious Planting Guidelines

Red Delicious apple trees will thrive best in soil that is well drained and not overly compacted. If your soil is heavy clay or has been heavily tamped down, your Red Delicious apple tree may do better in a raised bed. A raised bed should ideally be 1 ½' to around 2' wide, and about six feet wide to allow the roots to become established and to ensure proper drainage.

The Red Delicious tree will need a pollinator tree of a different variety. This second tree should be planted within 50' of the Red Delicious trees for the best pollination.

Soak the roots of the Red Delicious apple tree in water for about three to four hours before planting. The hole should be dug large enough that the root system can be gently spread out; the root ball should be planted s that no roots are crossed or bent. For best results, plant the young tree at the depth that it was planted prior to your buying it. Fill the hole and firmly pat the soil down before watering the site again. A layer of mulch, between three to five inches deep and covering an area of two to three feet will help regulate temperature and moisture. Move the mulch away from the trunk of the tree so pests will not nest in it.

Maintenance:

Your young Red Delicious tree needs to be properly watered once a week, from rain or supplemental sources. It's important to note that too much watering is detrimental to the Red Delicious, too.

Six Month Health Check:

Thoroughly soak the planting site once per week to ensure the root system gets properly established.

One Year Health Check:

Your furry neighbors may start to take an interest in your Red Delicious apple tree, especially rabbits and deer. If you see them around your tree, you may need to place a fence around it that is about 3' to 4' in diameter and around 48" high.

***

THE MCINTOSH

Size at Maturity:

12 to 15' in height and 12-15' in width

Growing Climates:

The McIntosh apple is popular for growing in colder climates. They can be found in Eastern Canada, the Great Lakes, and throughout the northeast.

Expected Yield Season:

Fall through early winter

***

In 1811, farmer John McIntosh discovered the apple that would come to bear his family name while he was clearing some land. While it isn't entirely clear where the variety came from, the McIntosh seems to be related to the Snow apple (Fameuse).

McIntosh apples have a soft skin with very tender flesh. The taste is sweet, with just a hint of an acidic tang. They are very versatile for using in fruit salads, making applesauce, or eating fresh from the tree. They aren't good for baking, though, as they will collapse in the oven.

McIntosh Planting Guidelines

McIntosh apple trees prefer full sun and soil with excellent drainage. Before planting your tree, make sure the roots are thoroughly moistened by placing their roots in water for about a day.

The hole needed for the McIntosh apple tree will be about two feet deep and twice the tree's diameter. Before covering the roots, spread them gently out in the hole. Make sure as you are filling in the soil around the tree that the graft remains exposed. Finish planting the tree by firmly pushing down the soil around it to push out air pockets.

Lay a cover of mulch or organic material in a circle of around 3 feet, keeping it away from the trunk of the tree.

Maintenance

Once established, the McIntosh apple tree is low maintenance and very hardy.

Six Month Health Check

Apple trees need to be cross-pollinated with a crabapple variety to produce fruit.

Fertilize young trees up to three times a year.

Prune and trim to give the tree a strong framework, focusing on scaffold branches.

One Year Health Check

The McIntosh apple tree will continue to grow at moderate rates and will be about 15' (5m) at maturity.

Look for the tree to fill with white blossoms in the spring, from early to mid-May

Fruit will be ready to harvest by the fall, mid to late September

When weather is dry, water your McIntosh apple tree twice a week

***

PINK LADY

Size at Maturity:

20' tall by 15' wide

Growing Climates:

In the states, California and Washington are prime. It is also grown in fifteen other countries.

Expected Yield Season:

Late fall through the spring

***

The Pink Lady is trademarked for its great taste. Australia calls this variety the number one apple in the country.

The Pink Lady is the perfect balance of sweetness with a hint of tartness, and is a very crunchy, firm variety of apple that is paired with cheeses, eaten fresh off the tree, and baked into pies. It is a cross between the Lady Williams and the Golden Delicious apple varieties. An apple is only considered to be a Pink Lady if it meets strict standards for its acidic and sugar levels and has the right coloration. Over half a season's yield will be considered substandard and sold as an off-brand variety.

Pink Lady Planting Guidelines

Pink Lady stalks are only available through an authorized distributor. These trees require very specific care, such as the length of time the fruit must stay on the tree before harvesting, proper spacing between trees, and frequent pruning.

In the South, Pink Lady apple trees can be planted in the fall because the climate is mild and moist, giving the roots a chance to establish themselves before the spring. In the north, planting should wait until early spring.

The hole required for a Pink Lady will be about one foot deeper and one foot wider than the ball of the roots. Partially fill the hole with compost or other organic topsoil, then secure the tree to a stake placed downwind from the tree to support it as it grows.

Maintenance:

For the tastiest fruit, Pink Lady apples should be left on the tree for 200 days before picking.

Six Month Health Check:

Make sure the remains one inch above the soil level so the upper variety doesn't dominate the rootstock.

One Year Health Check:

Keep your Pink Lady apple tree supported with its trellis.

***

CRIPPS PINK APPLES

Size at Maturity:

30' in height by 15' wide

Growing Climates:

Washington State and Australia

Expected Yield Season:

Mid October through December

***

If a Pink Lady apple fails to meet industry standards, it is classified as a Cripps Pink apple. These apples have the same balance of sweetness and tartness as the Pink Lady and is called the Queen of Apples. Cripps Pink apples came to the Australian marketplace around 1985, making the journey to America during the 1990's.

Cripps Pink apples have an excellent shelf life if kept cold, up to three months, and their flavor is enhanced by being kept refrigerated for a month prior to consumption. It's recommended that a Cripps Pink apple be taken from cold storage for an hour before it's eaten to really bring out the flavor. This variety of apple will also keep well at room temperatures for about two weeks.

The Cripps Pink apple is excellent for a large variety of use in the kitchen. Its naturally sweet flavor makes it a popular choice for baking in pies and making applesauce. Because the Cripps Pink apple is resistant to browning after being sliced, it's a great choice for eating fresh or for adding to a cheese platter.

Cripps Pink Apple Tree Planting Guidelines

Cripps Pink apple trees will thrive if planted in organic or composted soils. Dirt that is too coarse or sandy may drain too quickly for your young tree to get the proper amount of water it needs.

Plant your Cripps Pink apple tree so that the upper part of its root ball, called the root crown, creates a shallow mound above the soil line to ensure it receives the water it needs whiling draining excess moisture. If preferred, plant the tree in a raised bed to stop the erosion of its root mound.

Maintenance:

Cripps Pink apple trees prefer to be in direct sunlight for at least six hours a day.

Six Month Health Check:

Make sure your tree continues to get enough water while also monitoring it for signs that the root mound is retaining too much moisture.

One Year Health Check:

Once the tree is established, you can start using nitrogen light fertilizers. Too much nitrogen will make the tree grow too fast, requiring constant pruning, but reduce the quantity of fruit on the branches. Pink Cripps apple trees will need fertilizers that have high contents of iron, potash, and phosphorous to thrive.

***

AMBROSIA APPLES

Size at Maturity:

10 to 20 feet high, 4 to 5 feet wide

Growing Climates:

By licensed growers in New Zealand, United States, Chile, Canada, and Europe

Expected Yield Season:

Late September through early October

***

The Ambrosia apple, named because it is sweet enough to be "the food of the gods," was first discovered in the 1990's in British Columbia's Similkameen Valley. Orchard owner Wilfrid Mennell discovered the chance seedling, and when his family found it to be an exceptionally flavorful and colorful variety, they placed a patent on the fruit.

Fortunately or unfortunately, this particular variety can currently only be grown by licensed growers under the regulation of the Okanagan Plant Improvement Corporation (PICO) to ensure all Ambrosia apples adhere to tough standards of color and flavor, but that patent will soon be running out in the United States.

A conical shaped apple with a unique two-colored skin, Ambrosia apples feature low acidity and honey sweet flavor. Accepted colors for this variety is a golden yellow colored base and a red or pink color throughout the rest of the apple.

The Ambrosia apple is preferred for kitchen use because it is sweet enough to eat fresh off the tree but holds its flavor and shape when baked into pastries, pies and tarts. They are an excellent choice for baked apples, and are moist enough to add flair to doughnuts, cake and muffins. The versatile Ambrosia apple is excellent sliced into rice and couscous or used as a savory roast along with root vegetables.

Ambrosia Apple Tree Planting Guidelines

Ambrosia apple trees are best planted when they are dormant. The trees need to be cared for as soon as they are received from the nursery and their roots allowed to soak from six to twelve hours before planting. The soil should not be overly moist when the tree is planted; if the soil is wet, the tree can be "heeled" by putting it into an open trench along the north facing side of a building. The trench should be deep enough to cover the roots. After planting, thoroughly soak the site with water.

Before planting the Ambrosia apple tree, carefully prune back any branches that appear to be broken using pruning shears or a sharp knife. Do not prune the root system at all.

Maintenance:

Ambrosia apples have a very short time for optimal harvest, so they must be monitored for several weeks before the expected yield dates.

Six Month Health Check:

Keep a three-foot diameter weed-free clearing around your Ambrosia apple tree so the weeds do not take away nutrients and moisture from the tree during its growth.

One Year Health Check:

Maintain the weed barrier and place mulch for weed control and to keep the tree moist.

***

CRISPIN (MUTSU) APPLES

Size at Maturity:

10' to 22' feet depending on the variety chosen

Growing Climates:

World wide

Expected Yield Season:

October and November

***

The Crispin apple is called Japan's Million Dollar Apple. The Mutsu apple was first created at the Aomori Research Institute sometime in the 1930's. In the 1940's, the Mutsu apple made it's appearance in the United States and the United Kingdom and was renamed the Crispin apple.

In the produce aisle, the Crispin is one of the pricier varieties due to its flavor and versatility. This firm apple features a yellow or bright green coloration and a unique taste blend of sweet, tart, and subtle spice.

Crispin apples are commonly used in a variety of ways in the kitchen. Considered a dessert apple, it can be served stuffed, fried, made into a tasty applesauce, or baked into pies, tarts and muffins. Harvested Crispin apples can be kept for long periods of time in cold storage; cold storage releases even more flavor and sweetness.

Crispin Planting Guidelines

Crispin apple trees prefer to be planted in the fall. They will thrive in regular garden soil and don't require specific potting soil or composting materials unless your soil is heavy clay.

Place the root ball into the hole and make sure to pat the soil firmly back into place. Professional growers will leave the soil lower around the trunk of the tree to collect rainwater.

If you have clay soil, it should be mixed with organic materials.

Your tree should only have three or four branches at this time; remove any extra growth.

Maintenance:

When pruning, don't remove the stubby spurs from branches. These will be the first to yield fruit.

Six Month Health Check:

The Crispin apple tree will continue to grow over the winter if planted in the fall. Make sure the young tree has a mulch layer to protect it from freezes.

One Year Health Check:

Prune your Crispin apple tree in the spring to allow light to reach all the branches. Be sure to remove limbs that are broken, dead, crossed, or rubbing on other limbs.

***

BRAEBURN APPLES

Size at Maturity:

15' tall by 15' wide

Growing Climates:

Across the United States, except for states that get very cold such as New England and the norther Midwestern states. They have become one of the top apples produced in Washington state and New Zealand

Expected Yield Season:

Late fall through early spring

***

The Braeburn apple is a naturally occurring apple, not a cultivar. In 1952, they were found in the Braeburn Orchard of New Zealand and are currently one of the most produced apples in that country. The Braeburn apple keeps very well and is highly resistant to shipping damage. It can be safely refrigerated for up to a month.

A relatively new apple variety, Braeburn apples is a versatile variety known for its classic apple taste, both tart and sweet, along with subtle hints of cinnamon and nutmeg.

Braeburn apples are best fresh off the tree, and they produce very few juices when baked.

Braeburn Apple Tree Planting Guidelines

Braeburn apple trees prefer a sheltered site away from frost pockets. A high location in full sun with deep, well drained soil is ideal.

Braeburn apple trees like to be planted at a depth no deeper than its root ball but with a width at least three times bigger than the root system's diameter. Gently spread the roots when planting, and it the walls of the hole are too firm, loosen them before planting the young tree.

Maintenance:

The Braeburn apple tree will require supplemental watering.

Six Month Health Check:

Your Braeburn apple tree needs some corrective pruning while it is young. Focus on removing any branches that are broken, diseased and unhealthy, or dead.

One Year Health Check:

Make sure the tree is getting enough water. Even though the surface of the soil seems moist, the roots may still be dry. Frequent watering of the young tree will avoid drought stress, even if the summer has been cool and moist.

Monitor your Braeburn apple tree and remove any side shoots, known as lower laterals, growing on the trunk.

***

GRANNY SMITH APPLES

Size at Maturity:

12' to 16' in height by 10' to 14' wide

Growing Climates:

Below the Mason-Dixon line in the United States

Expected Yield Season:

November and December

***

The Granny Smith apple was originally an Australian apple cultivar named after Maria Anne Smith who created it. This apple is quite tart and the variety resists browning after being sliced far longer than other varieties.

The Granny Smith apple is juicy and firm with a distinctly tart taste, full of very subtle sweetness that will be more apparent if the apple is kept in cold storage. It is a bright green apple, often found with whitish speckles on its thick skin. In colder climates, the apples may be pinkish or yellow.

The Granny Smith apple is very versatile in the kitchen, often used in applesauce, cheese platters, stuffing, pancakes, as well as eaten fresh. They are excellent for baking pies because they have a high acidic content and keep their shape during baking.

Granny Smith Apple Tree Planting Guidelines

All weeds need to be removed from the planting site, making sure you remove them at the root level so they don't grow back. While the Granny Smith apple tree grows in a wide variety of dirt, mixing some organic material into the soil is a good way to ensure the tree thrives.

When planting, avoid locations where any older fruit trees have been removed recently.

Maintenance:

Keep your Granny Apple tree safe from furry pests by protecting the trunks with commercial tree guards or wire netting material.

Six Month Health Check:

Monitor your trellis to make sure the ties you are using aren't cutting into the tree itself. Once the roots are established, usually after two years, you can safely remove the trellis.

One Year Health Check:

Make sure your Granny Smith apple tree is watered regularly throughout the year. Once the tree blossoms, feed the tree tomato food or any other feed that is high in potash to encourage healthy fruits and flowering.

**

CAMEO APPLES

Size at Maturity:

Between 12' to 20' tall and 12' to 20' wide, depending on the variety chosen

Growing Climates:

Across the United States, mostly centered in Washington State. Cameos are also gaining popularity in Great Britain and are mostly produced in Kent, England

Expected Yield Season:

March through early June

***

The Cameo apple is a new name for the classic Carousel apple that was found in a Wenatchee orchard in Washington state in the 1980's. Cameo apples that come from Washington state must adhere to standards of color, taste and texture as set forth by the Cameo Apple Marketing Association, or CAMA. The Cameo is thought to be related to both Red and Golden Delicious varieties of apple.

Cameo apples are known for having a delicate, thin skin and juicy crisp texture. They are a great balance of tartness and sweetness with subtle tastes of citrus and honey.

Being resistant to browning after slicing, the Cameo is a popular variety of apple for salads, cheese platters, garnishing, and sandwiches. The Cameo's flavorful sweetness is increased when the apple is used in pies and other baked goods, and they maintain their shape while cooking. Cameos are frequently used in cobblers, polenta and quiche.

Cameo Apple Tree Planting Guidelines

Cameo apple trees will thrive if phosphate is added to the hole at the time of planting. Gently spread the root system out and place them around a small cone of dirt at the bottom of the hole. Add soil until the root system is covered to a depth of 3", then press firmly on the dirt. Add more phosphate before completely covering your young tree.

The trunk bend immediately above the graft should point north or northeast to protect it from heat stress and sunburned bark.

Maintenance:

Cameo apples will develop stripes when they are ready to be harvested.

Six Month Health Check:

Protect the Cameo's bark from sunburn by painting the tree with a fifty-fifty mix of water based flat interior paint and water, all the way to the ground.

One Year Health Check:

Keep accurate, detailed lists of the trees in your orchard even if you only have a few. This information is valuable for communicating with any one who might need to understand your tree varieties. Don't rely exclusively on tree tags; these are unreliable and may tear off. Your files should include:

- Cultivar

- Tree's location

- Rootstock

***

HONEYCRISP APPLES

Size at Maturity:

12' to 15' high and 12' to 15' wide

Growing Climates:

New England and Northern Great Lakes States

Expected Yield Season:

Mid-August through September

***

The Honeycrisp was named the official state fruit of Minnesota in 2006. These apples are known for their unique colorations featuring a yellow background and a reddish or pink blush over the entire surface.

They have a crisp, slightly crunchy texture that is slightly sweeter than it is tart. Its sweetness will increase even more as it ripens. Honeycrisp apples taste best when eaten a week after being in cold storage; by the time they appear on a grocer's produce shelf, they are at optimum flavor. When growing them at home, you can refrigerate them after harvesting.

Honeycrisp apples are perfect for any kitchen use including pies, applesauce, fruit salads and cheese platters.

Honeycrisp Apple Tree Planting Guidelines

Honeycrisp apple trees enjoy full sunlight. When planting your young tree, you may want to boost its chances for establishing a healthy root system by sprinkling them with mycorrhizal fungi if the quality of your soil is poor. It's not necessary to fertilize your tree when you first plant it.

Maintenance:

It's important to monitor the tree for any dead foliage that may be indicating drought stress, but by the time you see the signs it may be too late. Setting up an irrigation schedule is important with the Honeycrisp apple tree. Any weather conditions that are dry or overly windy can lead to a shortage of water for the tree.

Six Month Health Check:

Ensure your Honeycrisp apple tree is getting enough water by equipping them with watering bags or other watering aids, especially when the tree is newly planted. You can find irrigation tubes at any local home improvement store. Some tubes are made of biodegradable materials such as corn starch.

One Year Health Check:

While too little water is bad for your Honeycrisp apple tree, overwatering is harmful as well. If your soil has poor drainage, overuse of automatic irrigation systems can lead to rotting roots. The signs of rotting roots are similar to those seen in drought stress. To make sure your tree is drying properly between waterings, use a trowel to dig down to the root ball to make sure it is dry before watering it again.

***

PAULA RED APPLES

Size at Maturity:

10' to 20' in height by 10' to 20' in width, depending on the variety chosen

Growing Climates:

Across the United States

Expected Yield Season:

Late August through mid-October

***

Paula Red apples, named after the wife of Lewis Arrends who discovered the apple as a chance seedling, were found in Sparta, Michigan in 1960. Since their introduction to the market in 1968, they have been growing in popularity and are currently one of the most eaten apple varieties throughout the United States. The Paula Red apple is a favorite variety for kids and teens, from ages 2 to 19, and a popular source of apple juices. They are one of the first apple varieties to yield during the early fall. Paula Reds seem to be related to McIntosh apples, but the origin of this variety is not entirely clear; it is thought that the Cortland apple is also related to Paula Reds.

Paula Red apples look like McIntosh apples, with a dusty red skin under gold speckles. Their taste is a good balance of sweetness and tartness.

Paula red apples are tasty to eat fresh, but they are average for cooking and baking purposes. To get tasty pies, combine Paula Red with apples that maintain their shape when cooking. Paula Red apples are great for applesauce, but unless they are used immediately after harvesting they will lose their firmness, become mealier, and taste sweeter after storing them.

Paula Red Apple Tree Planting Guidelines

To ensure your soil is protected from heavy rain and the formation of impermeable crusts, plant weeds and ryegrass for stabilization. When it's time to plant your Paula Red apple tree, kill off the weeds and grasses so they don't compete for valuable nutrients and water with your young tree. The roots of the dead weeds and grasses will improve the structure of the soil.

Maintenance:

Sending your soil for testing will show you if you have any layers that are too hard to promote proper circulation of air and water, or that will keep the roots from taking hold in deeper layers. If your soil is acidic, measuring 5.7 or under, you may need to add lime to it. Unless you've applied superphosphate to the soil, you may also need to add phosphorous; if the soil test shows proper levels of soluble phosphorus you can skip this step.

Six Month Health Check:

Your objective now is to maintain proper pruning of your growing tree's branches. Neglecting them results in delayed fruiting and poor growth. When pruning your Paula Red apple tree, your focus should be on removing unwanted branches and controlling the shape of those that remain for a well-balanced, strong framework of scaffolding branches.

One Year Health Check:

After the first growing season, you should see the development of healthy branches. Clothes pinning them earlier should have resulted in wide angles. As this point, the focus is on developing a framework of good scaffolding branches and a strong central leader.

***

EMPIRE APPLES

Size at Maturity:

12' to 16' high by 12' to 6' wide

Growing Climates:

Mostly in the Northeast and upper Midwestern states.

Expected Yield Season:

Mid-September through the end of November

***

Empire apples originated in 1945 in Geneva, New York. They were widely introduced across the states in 1966. This sturdy apple tree is disease resistant, making it a hardy choice for hobby and professional growers alike.

Empire apples are a beautiful bright red and feature some light white and greenish color variations on the skin. It is a crisp apple, with the sweetness of a Red Delicious and the tartness of a McIntosh.

Empire apples are delicious raw and is one of the varieties preferred for baking and cooking. They are popular lunch box snacks, tasty in coleslaws or with chicken, and sliced into salads. They are especially tasty when paired with spices like nutmeg, ginger and cinnamon. They are perfect for cheese platters and pair very well with pear and pumpkin.

Empire Apple Tree Planting Guidelines

Before planting your Empire apple tree, loosen the sides of the hole with a fork or hand rake to encourage its roots to spread out and firmly establish themselves. A trellis is a good option for stabilization but take care when driving it into the ground that you avoid the roots of your young tree so they aren't damaged.

Gently spread the roots out after putting the tree in the ground. Add soil, tamping it down firmly as you fill the hole. When the tree resists being uprooted as you pull it, it's planted firmly enough to grow well.

Maintenance:

After planting, water the site well. Adding a layer of mulch helps to seal in moisture and add protection from freezing and frost. Make sure to keep the mulch from lying directly against the tree to discourage rodents from nesting in it and snacking on the bark of your tree.

Six Month Health Check:

Check on your trellis, and make sure the strings and ties aren't cutting into the tree. Make sure the ties are attached firmly while still allowing some movement.

One Year Health Check:

Keep actively pruning your Empire apple tree to train it to grow up and out for five years or so. Thin out any branches that are damaged or crossed. After five years, the tree should be pruned only during the dormant season.

***

JAZZ APPLES

Size at Maturity:

Varies

Growing Climates:

Global

Expected Yield Season:

Late September through April

***

In New Zealand during the 1980's, Allen White of the Plant and Food Research at Havelock North developed the Jazz apple. Commercial production began late in the 1990's in New Zealand before spreading across the globe in 2010. The Jazz apple is also known as the Scifresh apple and is currently patented and controlled by ENZA, the New Zealand Apple and Pear Marketing Board. The dual colored Jazz apple is a cross of the Royal Gala and Braeburn apple varieties.

The Jazz apple is a round variety with rosy red bases and a splash of yellows, greens and oranges across the skin. It is very crisp and has a taste of sweetness and tartness combined with some hints of pear.

Jazz is a dessert apple that holds its texture and flavor when baked into pies, tarts, and galettes. It is a great choice for baked apples, bread, muffins and cakes and is a great addition to stuffing, chicken or vegetables in roasts.

Jazz Apple Tree Planting Guidelines

Jazz apple trees do well in holes that are dug to twice the size as their root balls, but they prefer a slightly shallower hole to discourage the tree from settling too deep. Loosen the soil on the walls of the hole to encourage the root system to branch out and establish itself firmly. Plant your Jazz apple tree in an area that will not collect rainwater.

Make a dirt mound or cone in the middle of the hole and spread the roots out gently over it before beginning to fill in the hole.

Maintenance:

Jazz apple trees don't do well when their roots are submerged, so it's important to keep an eye on the planting mound and add more dirt if necessary, encouraging excess water to run off the mound rather than drown the root system.

Six Month Health Check:

At this point, don't attach your Jazz apple tree to a trellis quite yet. It doesn't need any supplements like fertilizer or other additives, either; just keep up with watering it frequently. If you add a protective layer of mulch, pull it back from the trunk to discourage rodents from nesting in it, and make sure it is thin enough that water can get through it and to the root system.

One Year Health Check:

Prune your Jazz apple tree until it looks like a vase; remove the leader and any branches that are not going in the right direction. The focus of pruning at this stage is to let some side limbs grow and cut back the ends of scaffolding branches. Your young tree can be pruned at least three times a year from this point on, thinning the branches to open the center. You can cut new growth back by half in both the spring and the late summer.

***

YELLOW DELICIOUS APPLES

Size at Maturity:

20 to 25' feet tall by 25' wide for standard. Semi dwarf trees range from 12 to 15' tall and 12 to 15' wide, with dwarf trees averaging 10' tall and 10' wide.

Growing Climates:

Across the United States

Expected Yield Season:

Late September through December

***

Yellow Delicious apples were first discovered in Clay County, West Virginia. They were named as the state's official fruit in 1995. An Italian led research group announced in 2010 that it had completely decoded the genome of this apple variety, reporting that it had 57,000 genes. The Yellow Delicious apple has the highest number of genomes of any other plant species. It consistently places in the top fifteen favorite apple cultivars across the United States.

Yellow Delicious apples can vary in coloration from a pale green to a rich gold and most often feature small spots on their skins. This medium sized apple is conically shaped and are very crisp and firm. They have a honey taste and a great balance of sweetness and tartness. It tastes very similar to the Red Delicious apple variety. It is especially susceptible to shriveling and bruising when being stored.

The Yellow Delicious apple is a favorite for baking pies and other desserts and is refreshing when eaten fresh or sliced into salads.

Yellow Delicious Apple Tree Planting Guidelines

Yellow Delicious apple trees require a moderately rich soil that provides adequate drainage and promotes air circulation around the root system.

Your planting hole should be a foot deeper and twice the root ball's diameter, taking care that you keep the scion 2" to 3" above the soil level when the hole is filled in. Tamp the soil and add water as you refill the hole, and finish with a mulch layer of around 2" to 4" to retain moisture and deter weed growth.

Maintenance:

The Yellow Delicious apple requires six or more hours of direct sunlight to encourage fruiting.

Yellow Delicious apple trees are very susceptible to insects and disease. Choose a variety that is resistant to both, or you may find yourself committing to spraying the tree frequently.

Six Month Health Check:

Apply a layer of mulch to retain moisture and give the tree protection against freezing and frost. Make sure the mulch doesn't touch the tree's trunk to keep rodents and other pests from nesting in the mulch and eating the bark of the tree.

One Year Health Check:

Most Yellow Delicious apple trees will need to be routinely sprayed every two weeks to repel fungus and destructive insects.

***

GALA APPLES

Size at Maturity:

20' to 25' high by 25' wide.

Growing Climates:

Throughout the Central and Northern United States and the northern points of most southern states.

Expected Yield Season:

July through September

***

In the 1930's, a professional apple grower named J.H. Kidd from New Zealand crossed Golden Delicious with Kidd's Orange Red apples to create the now widely popular Gala apple variety. The Gala apple cultivar was patented in 1974 in the United States. The United Kingdom first produced the apples several years later in the 1980's.

The Gala apple covers many sub-varieties, each with unique colorations and characteristics. The original Gala apple had an orange hued skin with orange stripes across the apple. The Gala apple variety features thin skin with a flesh that is juicy, crisp, aromatic and very sweet.

Gala apples are popular choices in applesauce and juices as well as cheese and fruit platters. They are good for baking and slicing into salads or very refreshing when eaten fresh.

Gala Apple Tree Planting Guidelines

The Gala apple tree doesn't require being planted deeply in its hole. In fact, planting the tree too deeply can have negative effects on your tree, causing it to become unhealthy and eventually die off altogether. The top of the root ball should never be lower than the soil level itself.

If you have determined that your soil quality is poor, mix compost or organic soil into your fill dirt to give your Gala apple tree a better chance of establishing a healthy root system. Generally, it isn't advisable to add fertilizer when planting your tree.

Maintenance:

The Gala apple tree is not resistant to drought and will grow best in soil that retains moisture while allowing excellent water drainage.

Six Month Health Check:

If you added organic soil or compost to the planting soil, microorganisms in the soil will encourage these additives to break down for the proper release of nutrients. You can choose to add a slow-release fertilizer if it is organically based.

One Year Health Check:

Your tree should be recovering from the initial shock of transplanting and is better able to absorb nutrients now. You can purchase mycorrhizal fungus, a natural and beneficial fungus variety, from any gardening supply store. Mycorrhizal fungus will attach itself to the roots of your tree and help them collect nutrients and water from the soil.

***

FUJI APPLES

Size at Maturity:

Standard trees will reach a height of between 20' to 25' high and 25' wide. The semi-dwarf tree will reach 12' to 15' in height and 12' to 15' in width. A dwarf tree will grow to around 10' high and 10' wide

Growing Climates:

Across the central United States

Expected Yield Season:

Mid-September to mid-October

***

The Fuji apple was developed at the Tohoku Research Station in the late 1930's in Aomori, Japan. This hybrid is a cross of the Old Virginia Ralls Genet and Red Delicious varieties. The Fuji apple got its name from the town where is was first developed, Fujisaki. The population of Japan still prefers the Fuji apple over all other varieties; as a result, they have very few apple imports in Japan. They were introduced to American consumers in the 1980's and are currently listed as one of the top fifteen most popular apple varieties in the states.

The Fuji apple is very large and can be stored for incredibly long periods of time; a refrigerated Fuji apple can stay fresh for a year. They are very crisp and dense and are among the sweetest apple varieties.

Fuji apples are popular for eating fresh and are also widely preferred for baked goods and pies. This flavorful variety is used in cheese and fruit platters and salads as well as applesauce.

Fuji Apple Tree Planting Guidelines

Fuji apple trees do best when planted in the fall or spring and will thrive in areas that have around six hours of full sunlight.

Fuji apple trees do best in soils with pH levels of 6.0 to 7.0. It may be necessary to send soil samples to test these levels as well as to test levels of magnesium, calcium, nitrogen, phosphorus, and potassium.

Fuji apple trees require excellent drainage. You can test the drainage of your soil by filling a one-foot deep hole with water and letting it drain naturally. Once it is empty, refill it again while tracking the water levels when it is full. In 15 minutes, measure the water level again. If the water has drained between ¼ and ½ inch, your soil has acceptable drainage for your Fuji apple tree.

Soak your Fuji apple tree roots for between one to two hours prior to planting the tree. Select a location far from water pipes, patios or sidewalks to prevent the root system from damaging them.

Start planting your Fuji apple tree by digging a hole roughly two or three times as wide as the root ball with a depth of between 18' to 24'. Add your soil adjustments as needed and fill the hole with water. Once the water has drained, place the tree in the hole taking care that the scion is two to three inches above the soil level. Refill half of the hole and water again, allowing the soil to settle around the root system. Once the water has drained, you can fill the rest of the hole with soil and tamp the mound to release air and settle the dirt.

Maintenance:

Your Fuji apple tree will require pollination from a different variety of apple tree that shares the same blooming period. This tree should be planted about fifty feet from your Fuji apple tree.

Six Month Health Check:

Fuji apple trees should be trained to a central leader with its scaffolding branches evenly arranged around the tree. Pruning should be performed to encourage the growth of lateral branches with wide forks as well as to control the tree's height. Any heavy growth should be thinned out to improve the quality of the yield as well as to control pests and diseases. Fertilizer can be applied in early spring or late winter, with one pound of 10:10:10 fertilizer for every year since the tree has been planted, with a maximum of five or six pounds total.

One Year Health Check:

The Fuji apple tree is prone to several diseases including cedar apple rust, apple scab, fire blight, and powdery mildew. Trees should be routinely sprayed with an all-purpose fungicide just as their buds are beginning to open in the spring. In the winter, spray a horticultural oil to prevent mites and aphids over the winter months. Malathion insecticides are useful for controlling the codling moth, which will lead to worms in your apples. You can perform soil testing annually to be sure your tree is getting its proper nutrients.

***

JONAGOLD APPLES

Size at Maturity:

12' to 16' in height by 16' wide

Growing Climates:

World wide

Expected Yield Season:

Mid-September through mid-October

***

The Jonagold is an apple variety that is a cross between the Jonathan and Golden delicious apple varieties. It was developed in New York in 1953 in Cornell University's New York State Agricultural Experiment Station. They are very large in size, making them a popular choice of apple to grow around the world.

Jonagold apples are large and can range in color variations from a yellowish green to a rosy orange hue. It is covered in vertical stripes and red spots. Its colorations are largely dependent on its storage temperatures and the strain of apple.

The Jonagold is a perfect balance of tartness and sweetness under a very thin skin. It has a taste similar to honeydew melons and is crunchy and grainy. The Jonagold takes its honey taste from the Golden Delicious and its acidity from the Jonathan.

Jonagold apples are very popular in recipes. Theycan be baked into muffins, tarts, cakes and pies or used by themselves to prepare baked apples.

Jonagold Apple Tree Planting Guidelines

Jonagold apple trees prefer soil that is soft and well aerated, so tilling is recommended before planting your young tree. If your soil is hard, mix a five-gallon bag of gardening or potting soil onto the dirt prior to tilling it to mix it in your existing dirt.

Jonagold apple trees prefer soil with a pH level of 6.5.

Maintenance:

The Jonagold requires other apple tree varieties within fifty feet of it to encourage pollination and increase your tree's apple yield.

Six Month Health Check:

During weeks or limited rainfall and drought, water your Jonagold apple tree until the ground is soaked up to one inch in depth.

One Year Health Check:

Make sure to maintain a circle of around four feet in diameter that is completely cleared of weeds and other vegetation for at least three years after planting. You can lay a ring of mulch but be sure to keep the mulch away from the trunk of your tree.

***

MACOUN APPLES

Size at Maturity:

12' to 16' in height by 16' wide for standard trees. Dwarf trees range from 8' to 12' tall and 12' wide

Growing Climates:

Cooler states in the north-eastern United States

Expected Yield Season:

Fall through early winter

***

Macoun apples are cultivars that have been derived from the Jersey Black and the McIntosh apple varieties. Some may pronounce this variety as "ma-coon," but the correct pronunciation is "ma-cow-an."

The popular Honeycrisp apple variety is widely believed to be descended from the Macoun, but genetic testing has proven that this isn't the case. This variety was discovered by a research team at the Geneva Research Station in New York in 1923, and named after a Canadian experimental apple grower, W.T. Macoun.

The Macoun apple is an irregularly shaped medium sized variety that ranges from almost black to a very deep red or purplish hue over a greenish skin, which may be visible at its stem. The crisp Macoun apple features a creamy white flesh that is very sweet, mixed with subtle hints of berries. Macoun apples have notoriously short storage lives and must be used within a week or two of harvest.

Because Macoun apples appear around the holidays, they are an excellent variety to use in holiday offerings from pies to sharp cheese platters and are popular in fresh salads. This variety is generally considered one of the most versatile cooking apples of all time. They make a great applesauce with needing any excess sugar to sweeten them. The Macoun is especially popular in New England as a fresh snack.

Macoun Apple Tree Planting Guidelines

Lime can take several years to move through the soil and reach your Macoun's root system. When planting your young tree, apply lime to a 10' by 10' area around the planting mound. Phosphorous may also be added in the same manner depending on the results of soil testing.

The holes should be dug to a width and depth where the roots, gently spread, will not be cramped or bent from their positions. Tamp the soil firmly around your planting mound, making sure the scion is two inches above the soil level. Don't fertilize your young Macoun tree after planting; wait until the young tree has received its first drenching rain.

Maintenance:

Use the clothes pinning technique on your young tree to encourage wide angles in your branches, especially on any shoots that are developing underneath the central leader.

Six Month Health Check:

Macoun apple trees require frequent pruning up to three times a year. In the winter, early summer and again in the late summer focus on removing all unhealthy or bent limbs and tip all terminals to encourage proper growth of the remaining branches.

One Year Health Check:

After pruning, the scaffolding branches should be below the central leader after pruning. Develop another layer of scaffolding limbs about 24' to 30' above the previously established scaffold during the tree's second growth season, and use the clothes pinning technique on new growth to encourage wide branch angles.

***

CORTLAND APPLES

Size at Maturity:

Most popular tree variety is the semi-dwarf, ranging from 15' to 20' in height and 20' in width.

Growing Climates:

Washington state, Canada, Oregon and the east coast of the United States. France and Poland also grow Cortland apples.

Expected Yield Season:

Mid-fall into early winter seasons

***

Cortland apples are the hybrid apple variety from a McIntosh and Ben Davis cross. The name Cortland is from the county in Geneva, New York where the cultivar was developed. This apple variety was first developed by a Cornell University professor, S.A. Beach at the New York State Agricultural Experiment Station in 1898. In 1915, it came to the general market and quickly became one of the most commonly produced apples in New York State. The Cortland apple has won several awards, such as the Wilder Medal of the American Pomological Society. Cortland apples are currently the twelfth most commonly produced apples throughout the United States.

Cortland apples range in size from medium to long and have a flat shape. They have a bright red coloration with dark streaks, and a greenish bush capping them. They are crisp with a very juicy sweet tart, sharp and vinous flavor.

The Cortland apple is excellent when cubed and added to fruit salads. They are also a popular choice to add, thinly sliced, to quesadillas, sandwiches and hamburgers. The Cortland apple is a good choice for cheese platters with dips or cheese. This variety is excellent for baked goods like tarts, galettes and quiche, cakes, pies and cobblers. They are a great choice for cider and apple juice as well as applesauce, preserves, and soups.

Cortland Apple Tree Planting Guidelines

The Cortland apple is a cold weather apple that will need to be kept cooler in the summer months.

Organic materials added to the planting hole will bind to sandy soil, allowing it to retain nutrients and moisture. These materials also break down clay soil and particles of silt to allow water to soak into the roots, helping them to spread and establish a healthy system. Cortland apples will need to be staked to encourage growth and protect the young tree from damaging wind and weather.

Maintenance:

For the Cortland apple tree to thrive, it will need feeder roots at the top of the soil to absorb nutrients and proper amounts of water. Surface soil should be soft, well-structured, stable, fertile, and provide excellent drainage.

Six Month Health Check:

Avoid gaps created by trees that are not firmly planted by securing them. A tree that sways in the wind will widen its planting hole, making a gap that will collect water at the root level and cause rot. If that happens the tree will become unhealthy and die. When a newly planted tree rocks back and forth, they develop "crowbar hole," and the tree can pull completely free of its hole.

One Year Health Check:

Maintain the trellis or stake of your young tree to keep it sturdy and safe from "crowbar hole" and to prevent it from being damaged during weather extremes. The tree should be secured for the first two years.

***

DIVA APPLES

Size at Maturity:

20' to 25' tall by 25' wide for standard trees. Semi-dwarf trees will range from 12' to 15' in height and 15' wide, while dwarf trees are 10' tall by 10' wide

Growing Climates:

Northern United States

Expected Yield Season:

Spring through summer months

***

Diva apples were developed in Hawkes Bay, New Zealand. They were originally only sold by Freshmax Exports and Mr. Apple, both New Zealand companies, until 2015 when the Giumarra Wenatachee Company of Washington state began selling them in North America. The Diva apple is offered in an organic variety as well as conventional apples; Diva apples must be grown without the use of synthetic pesticides to be considered organic. The name "Diva" references the Italian word for "goddess" and is the result of an apple marketing technique that gives apple varieties short and catchy names that are easy for consumers to remember.

Diva apples feature a yellow green skin that is almost entirely covered by bright red hues. They are a squat shaped medium sized apple with a slightly ridged texture. The Diva apple is sweet like a Fuji or Gala apple with a crispness of the Granny Smith apple. It is very juicy with subtle hints of vanilla and grapes. Diva apples have a unique taste beyond their slight acidity and sweetness.

The sweetness and unique taste characteristics of the Diva apple make it a great choice for snacking or a good addition to cheese platters. Diva apples are known for longevity when stored in refrigerators and are resistant to bruising.

Diva Apple Tree Planting Guidelines

Diva apple trees need soil that is sandy and well drained. They prefer full sunlight for vigorous growth and healthy, tasty harvests. Don't place your Diva apple tree in any place that is at risk for freezing, like a frost pocket.

The hole required for your Diva apple tree to establish a healthy root system will be about three times the size of its pot wide and have a depth as deep as its root ball. Mix the fill dirt with half aged mushroom compost, aged compost, manure or rotten bark. Your young tree will not require any fertilizer until the fall season.

Maintenance:

After your Diva apple tree has a healthy root system, it will require one inch of water a week.

Six Month Health Check:

At this stage of planting, its important that you maintain proper watering of your young tree. Light and airy soils will need to be watered twice a week while clay or heavy soils can be watered just once per week. As you water, soak the entire root system; this may take between forty to fifty minutes.

One Year Health Check:

You can paint your tree trunk with a mixture of 50% water and 50% flat interior latex paint to protect your tree from sunburn damages, particularly if you are planting in the southwestern states of the United States. The trees can be painted from the ground level to the top of the tree.

***

The Fruit Trees Book: Growing Apples

MORE HINTS FOR GROWING HEALTHY TREES

When you decide to plant apple trees, you are making a commitment to caring for them from their initial planting through the first year and many years beyond. Your reward for your hard work will be healthy apple crops season after season.

Your trees will not reach maturity and yield fruit for several years, but they still must be properly cared for while they grow and establish themselves. During this time, you will need to formatively prune the tree and provide the proper nutrients and water so they can thrive and protect them against bad weather, pests and diseases.

Pollinating Your Trees

Many apple trees require pollination before they will bear fruit and seeds. Pollination in natural settings is done by bees, birds and the wind. In backyard orchards like yours, it will need to be done by hand. You will need to use a pollen-sprayer, cotton swab or a small brush to move pollen grains from a tree to the pistil of another tree.

Controlling Pests

Rabbits and deer can't resist the bark and fruit of apple trees and find young tender trees very appetizing. They can quickly become a problem for the hobbyist and professional apple grower alike. Fencing can be a deterrent, but deer can jump a fence and rabbits can burrow under it. Mesh netting is a good alternative to repel these furry nuisances. Some larger orchards will use guard dogs to frighten away deer and rabbits. Avoid harsh repellents or lethal measures if possible.

Apple trees are especially susceptible to insects such as hoverfly larvae, lacewings, earwigs and beetles. Synthetic pesticides can control the problem, but they are not environmentally friendly. Organic pest control is safer for the environment.

During the warmer months, hornets and wasps may not be welcome around your fruit trees but they are very efficient predators.

When you plant apple trees, you should be familiar with the various diseases that can quickly devastate an orchard.

Fertilization

Apple trees can have very specific soil requirements. Every few years, you should take a sample of your soil to be sure it is still meeting your tree's needs. The trees will also require fertilizer from time to time to promote healthy growth and high-quality apples.

Grafts

Grafting is a technique used to ensure that certain desired apple trees can reliably grow. It involves attaching a scion, or cutting from a parent tree, to a more established and vigorous rootstock, or root system. This ensures that fruit will be the same as the that of the parent plant. Without grafting, pollination may introduce new genetic material to the seed, resulting in unreliable fruits. Another grafting method is attaching a bud from the desired tree to a growing tree in a technique called bud grafting. Bud grafting allows several varieties of apples to be attached to the same tree.

Proper Watering

Your apple tree will require proper watering and, depending on the variety, this could be as frequently as one a week. The soil should be thoroughly soaked up to two or three feet deep. To make this chore easier, you can consider a micro-irrigation system which will use micro-spray or a micro-sprinkler to trickle water directly onto the tree. Micro-irrigation will ensure your apple tree is getting the moisture it needs while keeping excess water from pooling and wetting the surrounding areas.

Protecting from Weather

Apple trees can be very susceptible to weather extremes.

Winter: Protect your trees from frost with frost fans. You can consider outdoor heaters for your tree if the weather is predicted to be colder than normal. Sprinkling water on the tree trunks can be beneficial during winter months. Don't place your apple tree in any low-lying location that is prone to frosting.

Spring or summer: Tree bark can become sunburned during the warmer months. To protect your tree, paint it from the ground level to the top with a 50/50 mis of water and interior flat white latex paint.

Year round: Stake your young trees to keep them straight and protected from high winds.

Orchard Restoration

Whether you are thinking of restoring an apple orchard that has fallen into disrepair or looking to reclaim an apple tree you have in the back yard, bringing it back to life will take dedication and commitment. Once the apple trees have become covered in weeds and scrub, they can stop producing and become just another tree in the wild. This will be a long-term process, but worth it in the end.

The first year: The trees will require careful pruning in small increments. Only up to 25% of the tree should be cut back initially. These early pruning should only focus on removing diseased limbs.

Following years: Pruning in subsequent years can target dead or decaying branches, especially those that are threatening the tree's stability. After the diseased, decayed or dead branches have been removed, you can shift your focus to restructuring the tree, paying attention to gradually opening the crown to allow for air and light to penetrate the interior of the tree.

Old, established trees are important historically and biologically; if you have them on your property, try to restore them if you can.

Pruning

Your apple trees will require pruning when they are young to form their shape to keep branches from growing on the lower part of the tree, about two meters from the ground for standard apple trees. Pruning at this time is focused formatively, training the branches around the developing central leader. Removing any competing branches will keep the central leader growing strong and straight. Lower branches will need to be shortened to only two or three buds long.

As the tree matures, pruning is required to remove all dead, damaged or diseased limbs and continuing to remove all branches below two meters to encourage the tree to develop a good, strong scaffold.

Harvesting the Apples

When choosing your apple tree, some considerations are the size of the tree, the climate zone best suited for your tree, disease resistance and upkeep. Another consideration is when you want to enjoy the fruits of your labor.

Apple varieties have specific times when they will ripen and be ready for harvesting. Some varieties have very short harvest times, and others may produce fruit for months. Some are ready in the late spring, while most will ripen in the fall months with a few staying productive through early winter.

You will know your apples will be ready to be picked when they can be easily separated from the branches with a gentle twist. Once picked, you can keep them fresh longer by wrapping them and placing them in a refrigerated storage location.

Final Thoughts on Healthy Apple Trees

Apple trees are beautiful additions to any yard and provide valuable crops for orchards. They bloom with beautiful, delicate and sweet-smelling flowers, provide shade and of course, are the source for nutritious, healthy snacks. They each have unique characteristics such as where they thrive and when they will ripen. Some require less maintenance than others and some tree varieties, such as semi-dwarf and dwarf, will be much smaller and easier to take care of then standard sized trees. Many are hardy and resistant to pests and diseases, but some will be high risk for developing devastating diseases.

All apples aren't necessarily good for all purposes. Many varieties are better used in baking than eaten fresh, and some can't be successfully cooked at all. Many are resistant to bruising and browning and can be stored almost indefinitely, while others have a very short shelf life.

Before investing your time, passion and money into your apple tree:

Research all varieties that do well in your climate zone.

Take a visit to a produce stand or orchard and try some different apple varieties to see which ones you enjoy.

Never be afraid to ask questions of professional growers; they are more than happy to lend a hand.

Have your soil tested to see what levels of nutrients it has; different apple trees have different requirements to thrive. You may need to adjust your soil to plant your tree.

Invest in proper tools, such as pruning shears and irrigation methods, to make maintenance a little easier.

Remember that your dedication and commitment will pay off in the end when you are reaping your rewards; fresh apples from your own tree for years to come.

Vas Blagodarskiy

ABOUT THE AUTHOR

I was born in Eastern Europe where I was raised until the age of 10. During the summers, I would visit my grandmother's apple orchard on the outskirts of the city. It was a three-month period of the year that I would always look forward to. Nothing compares to spending time in the sun and enjoying nature with friends in the neighborhood.

This apple orchard is where I learned to ride a bike. It's where my grandmother practiced reading, writing and math with me. It's where I earned my cuts and bruises; climbing trees, swinging on the swing, digging around in the dirt and just generally being a curious kid.

As I grew older, my appreciation for the craft of apple tree maintenance has grown. I decided to learn everything that I could about this fine art. It turns out it's both fun and rewarding to have your own orchard. Now, I want to bring that childhood joy to readers worldwide.

While there is much more to maintaining an orchard, this practical guide has just given you the foundation you need to successfully start your own garden. Even if you're operating in a tiny space.

Apple trees can be grown successfully in greenhouses, too! Although they typically thrive under the bare sun, there could be soil conditions or weather patterns that may lend themselves to greenhouses. But that's a topic worth a whole another book.

I hope you enjoyed this practical guide to growing healthy apples. Please remember to leave it a good review so others can discover this book for themselves.

Thank you.

Made in the USA
Columbia, SC
29 August 2018